HOW TO
Hold a Pencil

By

Megan Hirsch

Hirsch Indie Press
los angeles

www.MeganHirsch.com
www.HirschIndiePress.com

ISBN: 978-0-9841328-0-5

Printed in the USA.

For Tristan and Harrison

Things you will need:

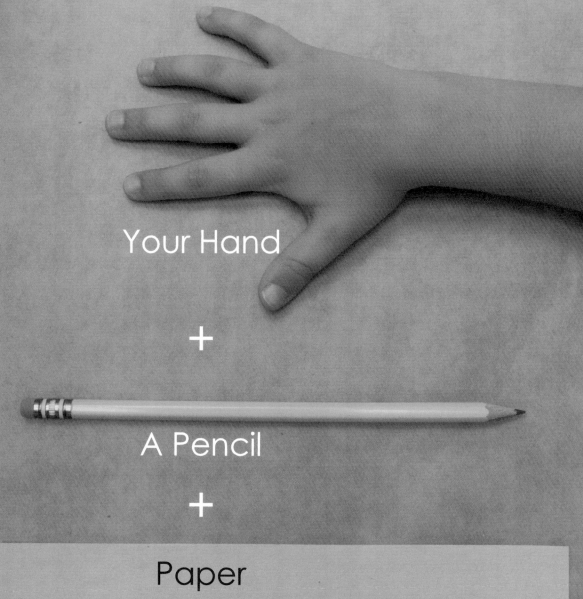

Your Hand

+

A Pencil

+

Paper

1.

First you pinch.

Then...

POINTER FINGER

THUMB

...bring up a friend
for support.

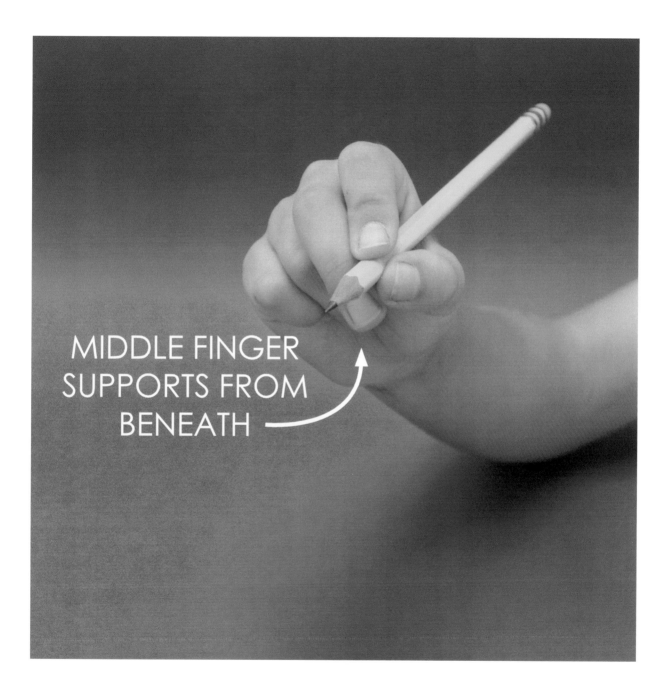

MIDDLE FINGER
SUPPORTS FROM
BENEATH

(This is what it looks like in the left hand.)

2.

Hold your fingers near the sharpened end...but not all the way to the tip.

ABOUT AN INCH
FROM THE TIP

This is too close to
the tip.

This is too far from the tip.

TOO FAR

3.

Your fingers should be bent a little bit (not too much and not too little).

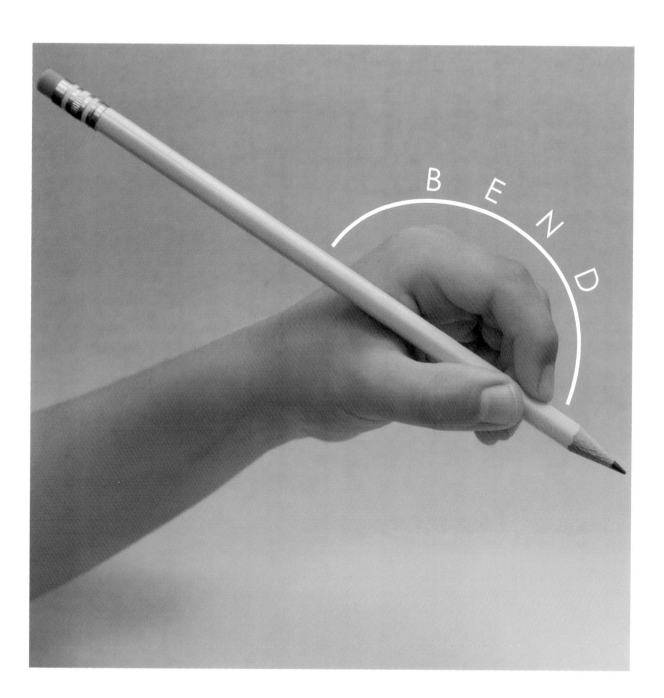

These fingers are

too bent.

These fingers are
too straight.

TOO STRAIGHT

4.

Press hard enough to see your work clearly.

This is pressing too hard.

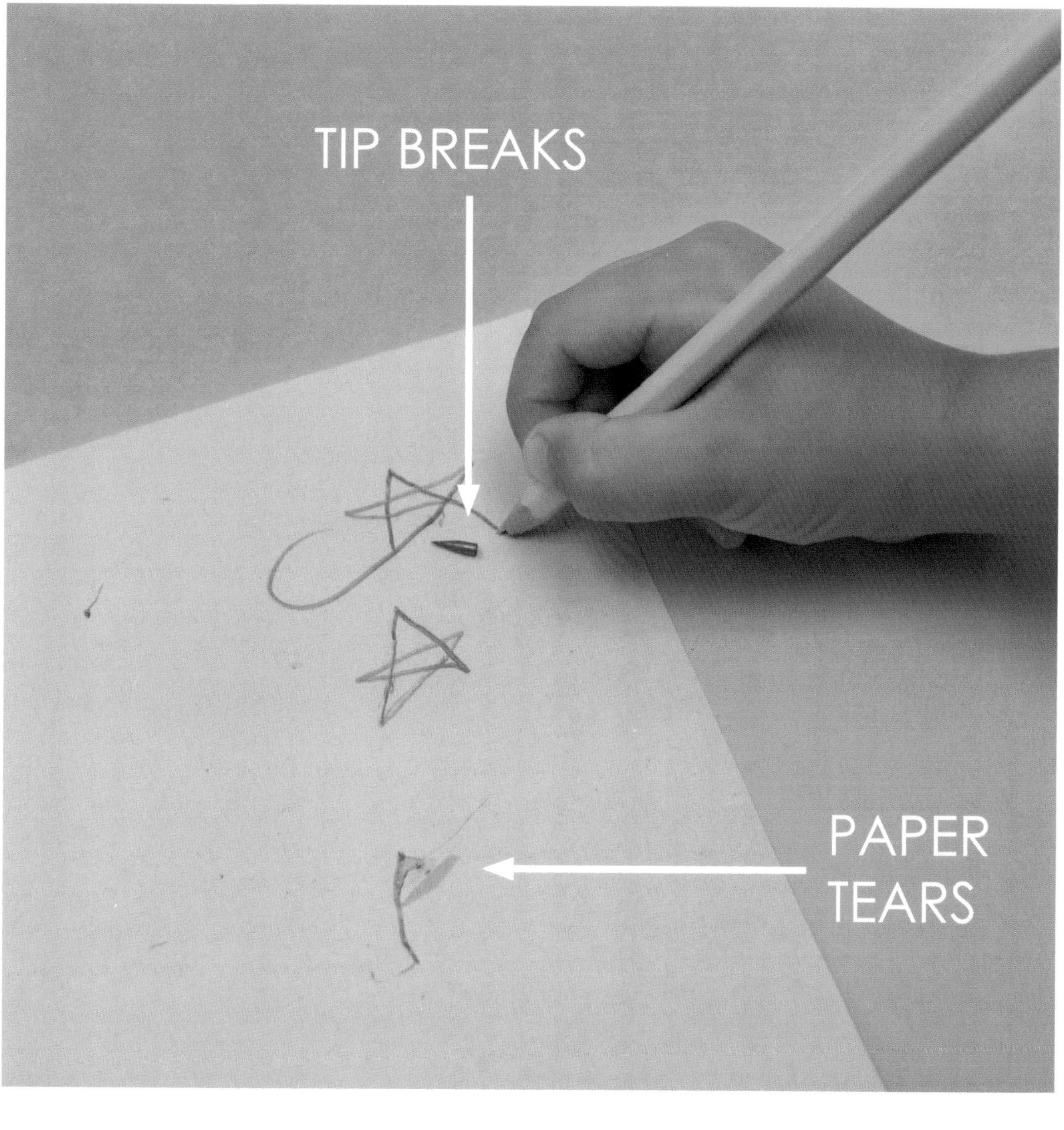
TIP BREAKS
PAPER
TEARS

This is pressing too softly.

Now you can hold all these other things, too!

CPSIA information can be obtained
at www.ICGtesting.com
Printed in the USA
LVIW010838290912

300629LV00002B